D1532556

To _____

From _____

Date _____

You're Always in My Heart

Photography copyright © 1997 by Virginia Dixon

Text copyright © 1997 by Garborg's Heart 'n Home, Inc.

Design by Thurber Creative

Published by Garborg's Heart 'n Home, Inc.

P.O. Box 20132, Bloomington, MN 55420

You're
Always In
My Heart

I thank God, my friend, for the blessing
you are...for the joy of your laughter,
the comfort of your prayers,
the warmth of your smile.

Everyone was meant to share God's all-
abiding love and care; He saw that we
would need to know a way to let these
feelings show. So God made hugs.

JILL WOLF

Blessed is the influence of one true,
loving human soul on another.

GEORGE ELIOT

Piglet sidled up to Pooh from behind.
"Pooh!" he whispered.
"Yes, Piglet?"
"Nothing," said Piglet, taking
Pooh's paw.
"I just wanted to be sure of you."

A.A. MILNE
THE HOUSE AT POOH CORNER

I always thank God for you.

1 CORINTHIANS 1:4 NIV

Thank you for the treasure of your
friendship. For showing me God's special
heart of love.

I said a prayer for you
And I know God must have heard,
I felt the answer in my heart
Although He spoke no word.
I asked that He'd be near you
At the start of each new day,
To grant you health and blessings
And friends to share the way.
I asked for happiness for you
In all things great and small,
But it was for His loving care
I prayed for most of all.

Oh, the comfort, the inexpressible comfort of feeling safe with a person: having neither to weigh thoughts nor measure words, but to pour them out.

GEORGE ELIOT

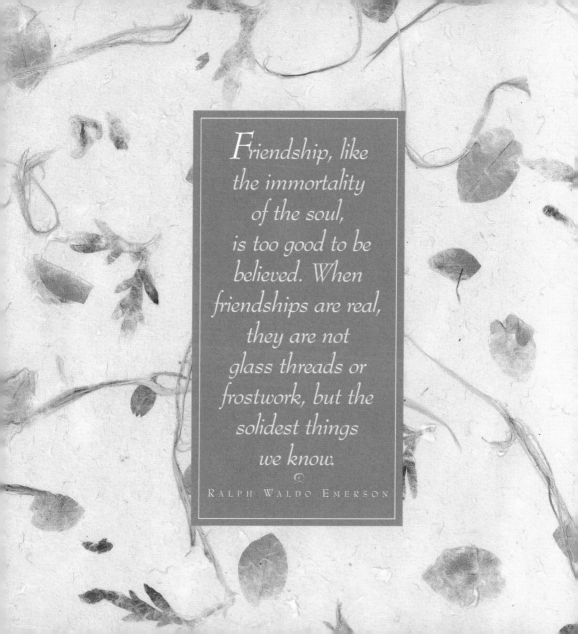

Friendship, like the immortality of the soul, is too good to be believed. When friendships are real, they are not glass threads or frostwork, but the solidest things we know.

RALPH WALDO EMERSON

You're my friend—what a thing
friendship is, world without end!

ROBERT BROWNING

What made us friends in the long ago
When we first met?
Well, I think I know;
The best in me and the best in you
Hailed each other because they knew
That always and always since life began
Our being friends was part of God's plan.

GEORGE WEBSTER DOUGLAS

One of life's greatest treasures is the love
that binds hearts together in friendship.

You are so special that once you entered
my life, it became richer and fuller and
more wonderful than I ever
thought it could be.

One friend ever watches and
cares for another.

RANDLE COSGRAVE

A friend is a person with whom I
may be sincere, before whom I
may think out loud.

RALPH WALDO EMERSON

Friends...they cherish each other's
hopes. They are kind to each
other's dreams.

HENRY DAVID THOREAU

Your best friend is the person who
brings out of you the best that is
within you.

HENRY FORD

Friendship is something that

It is the sort of love one can

I breathed a song

It fell on earth, I know

and the song

I found again in the heart

raised us almost above humanity...
imagine between angels. C. S. LEWIS

into the air;
not where...
from beginning to end,
of a friend. HENRY WADSWORTH LONGFELLOW

Life is fortified by many friendships. To love, and to be loved, is the greatest happiness of existence.

SYDNEY SMITH

I remember the times you were there for me, showing real interest and concern. I'm thankful for the closeness we share. How I enjoy being with you!

We don't need soft skies to make friendship a joy to us. What a heavenly thing it is; World without end, truly.... Such friends God has given me in this little life of mine!

CELIA THAXTER

My friend shall forever be my friend,
and reflect a ray of God to me.

HENRY DAVID THOREAU

I've written you in thoughts, my friend,
So often through the years,
But somehow ink just couldn't find
The words to make thoughts clear....
I've often written in my thoughts,
But here at last are words
To say I thank you for the joys
That in my heart you've stirred.

CRAIG E. SATHOFF

Being with you is like walking on a very
clear morning—definitely the sensation
of belonging there.

E. B. WHITE

How many, many springtimes
Have come and gone away;
But each one left a memory—
And memories will stay.

How many, many friendships
Life's path has let me see;
I've kept a scrap of each of them
To make the whole of me.

JUNE MASTERS BACHER

So wherever I am
there's always Pooh,
There's always Pooh
and Me.
"What would I do?"
I said to Pooh,
"If it wasn't for you,"
and Pooh said: "True,
It isn't much fun for
One, but Two can stick
together," says Pooh,
says he. "That's how it
is," says Pooh.

Two are better
than one...for if
they fall, one will
lift up the other.

ECCLESIASTES 4:9,10
NRSV

Hand grasps hand, eye
And great hearts expand
of this world's life.

What is a friend?   A single

I think of you often.
we always keep

lights eye in good friendship,
nd grow one in the sense

ROBERT BROWNING

soul dwelling in two bodies. ARISTOTLE

Whether we're near or far apart
each other in our hearts.

Can you measure the worth of a sunbeam,
The worth of a treasured smile,
The value of love and of giving,
The things that make life worthwhile?...
Can you measure the value of friendship,
Of knowing that someone is there,
Of faith and of hope and of courage,
A treasured and goodly share?
For nothing is higher in value,
Whatever life chooses to send—
We must prove that we, too, are worthy
And equal the worth of a friend.

GARNETT ANN SCHULTZ

I count your friendship one of
the chiefest pleasures of my life,
a comfort in time of doubt and
trouble, a joy in time of
prosperity and success, and
an inspiration at all times.

❦

EDWIN OSGOOD GROVER

Until we meet again, may God
hold you in the palm of His hand.

May the Lord watch between you
and me when we are absent one
from another.

❦

GENESIS 31:49 NKJV